CW01431611

Original title:
Cosmic Comedy Club

Author: Lila Davenport
ISBN HARDBACK: 978-1-80567-774-1
ISBN PAPERBACK: 978-1-80567-895-3

Galactic Giggles

A black hole's joke, it pulls you in,
It's hard to breathe, but let the laughs begin.
Aliens dance, they've got moves so sly,
In a rocket ship, we'll soar and fly.

Jupiter's moons, they wear a grin,
Spinning jokes where laughter's the din.
Saturn's rings have a playful sway,
Join the fun, let's sing and play!

Stars and Smiles

Stars wink down with a twinkling chuckle,
Mars in red, but still a soft snuggle.
Comets zoom by, with tails that tease,
"Catch me if you can!" they say with ease.

Asteroids tumble in a clumsy spree,
While the Milky Way hums a tune of glee.
Galaxies giggle as they spin around,
In this cosmic dance, joy can be found.

Laughter Among the Nebulas

Mist in the air, a colorful view,
Nebulas burst like a big laugh too.
Stars burst forth, bright and cheeky,
Making the night feel blissfully sneaky.

Cosmic jesters with a radiant glow,
Telling tales of the stars that flow.
In every corner where shadows might play,
Laughter ignites like a bright array.

Punchlines in the Cosmos

Punchlines echo in the vast unknown,
Where stardust whispers, we've brightly grown.
In orbit, the planets joke and tease,
The universe chuckles with effortless ease.

A supernova bursts with laughs and light,
Witty comets streak through the night.
Gravity bends but never the fun,
In this grand show, we're all on the run.

Comedic Constellations

Stars twinkle in giggles bright,
Their whispers tickle the dark of night.
Planets spin in a dance so odd,
Bouncing jokes with a cosmic nod.

Comets zipping, trails of glee,
Asteroids laugh as they roam free.
Galaxies swirl with humor divine,
In this universe, we all align.

Marauding Mirth in the Milky Way

Laughter echoes across the void,
As black holes munch, feeling overjoyed.
Supernovae burst with a chuckle so loud,
A star's bright laugh attracts a crowd.

Nebulas swirl like a cosmic breeze,
Tickling space with an endless tease.
From Venus to Mars, the giggles will sway,
In every corner, we jest and play.

Luminous Laughs

Radiant beams burst with a grin,
As light-years become a jesting spin.
Eclipses provide the punchline rich,
A game of tag with a time-warped pitch.

Jupiter's moons share tales of cheer,
With Saturn's rings that twinkle near.
The universe chuckles in harmonious strands,
While laughter resounds in stellar lands.

Space-Time Shenanigans

Warping through time with mirth on our side,
Wormholes giggle as we take a ride.
DistancesShrink, as jokes leap through,
Banter flies fast in this cosmic zoo.

Gravity pulls, but humor's our grace,
Each quasar's burst lights up the place.
In the fabric of time, we weave our fun,
Shenanigans under a glittering sun.

Cosmic Curiosity

In the vastness where laughter roams,
Aliens juggle in their funny homes.
Planets spin with quirky grace,
Stars twinkle in a playful race.

Asteroids dance with a wobble and sway,
Telling jokes that float away.
Black holes hiccup, stars burst in cheer,
Gravity doesn't hold back the glee here.

Fun on a Friendlier Planet

On a world where giggles bloom,
Spaceships zoom and share the room.
Martians in hats, with jokes to spare,
Invite you in for a cosmic affair.

Saturn's rings have a comedy show,
Where laughter is free and the tickets flow.
Neptune's whirlpool spins tales of delight,
As comets twirl, a merry sight.

Giggles in the Galaxy

Across the stars, in laughter we soar,
Jokes echo back from a distant shore.
Meteorites crack up with a gleeful sound,
While space dolphins frolic, joy unbound.

Celestial jesters perform with flair,
Tickling planets, spinning through air.
Nebulae shimmer with smiles so wide,
On this galactic fun-filled ride.

Starstruck Sillyness

Under the glow of a fizzling star,
Jokes are traded, both near and far.
Galaxies giggle, their swirl full of cheer,
As the universe tickles the ear.

Supernova pranks, in a colorful burst,
A fountain of laughter where we all thirst.
Comets parade, their tails full of fun,
In this cosmic comedy, we all are one.

Space Funk and Fun

In the void where stars align,
Jokes collide like space-time.
Aliens chuckle, asteroids wink,
Laughter spirals, don't you think?

Astro-nuts in shiny suits,
Bouncing through with silly boots.
Galactic giggles fill the air,
Gravity can't pull down despair.

Black holes with a twist of fate,
Swallowing punchlines, isn't that great?
Planetary puns dance like light,
In the twilight where dreams take flight.

With comets trailing jokes on paths,
Spreading joy like cosmic baths.
Dance with Saturn, moonwalk with Mars,
In this realm of whimsical stars.

Vortex of Laughter

In a swirl of jokes and fun,
We spin around, here comes the pun.
Gravity's grip can't hold us down,
As laughter echoes round and round.

Nebulae filled with gags galore,
Each starlit bellyache leaves us wanting more.
Falling into a humorous chase,
Warp speed to a comical place.

From meteors that joke and jest,
To supernovas that crack the best.
Wormholes lead to a chuckling spree,
Life's just better when we're carefree.

A cosmic jester on a grand stage,
Spreads the joy at every age.
Let's orbit around this light of glee,
In the whirl of laughter, wild and free.

Stellar Smiles

Stars twinkle with mischievous glare,
Together they share secrets rare.
With every grin, they ignite the skies,
Mapping joy where the humor lies.

Planets spin with a comic beat,
Each rotation brings laughter sweet.
Meteor showers, falling bright,
With giggles sparkling through the night.

Galaxies twist into banana peels,
Rolling laughter that truly heals.
In their embrace, we cast aside woes,
Amidst the rapture, laughter grows.

Celestial beings in vibrant suits,
Telling tales of goofy roots.
So spread the joy, let it compile,
We dance in the universe with stellar smiles.

Galactic Gags

In the depths of night, a jest takes flight,
In every corner, a giggle, a fright.
Planets humor, bright and bold,
Tales of clowns in space, retold.

Witty comets sliding past,
Each one leaving laughter cast.
Silly rockets zipped and zoomed,
In this realm, no one is doomed.

Superstars burst with humorous flair,
Tickling space from here to there.
Aliens bounce in a dance of delight,
Swapping puns under starlit night.

With every laugh, the stars align,
Creating joy that's truly divine.
In this vastness, let joy erupt,
As we gather here, our spirits up.

Laughter in the Cosmos

Stars twinkle with glee, / As comets all joke, / A
supernova's grin, / While black holes poke.

Galaxies spin, they jest, / Whirling with light, / Nebulas
burst in laughter, / A magnificent sight.

Planets roll on the floor, / Their moons join in the fun, /
Orbiting with chuckles, / 'Round the sun they run.

In this grand theater, / Space plays its part, / Where
laughter echoes, / And humor's an art.

Elysian Humor

Angels with wings of gold, / Share laughs in the air, /
With jokes that unfold, / Light as a prayer.

Clouds drift in delight, / Tickled by the breeze, / Lightning
bolts strike bright, / With punchlines that tease.

Flowers bloom with cheer, / Their petals aglow, / Even the
sun seems near, / With a radiant show.

In the fields of joy, / Laughter takes flight, / Elysium's
ploy, / In morning's first light.

Holo-Comic Hilarity

Pixels burst forth in glee, / As screens start to play, /
Virtual jesters sway, / In a hologram ballet.

Avatars giggle aloud, / Their antics en masse, / Creating a
digital crowd, / With humor that lasts.

From memes to bright gifs, / They dance in the air, /
Making us laugh in shifts, / Without a single care.

In this pixel parade, / Laughter fills the void, / A
holographic charade, / Where smiles can't be destroyed.

Gravitational Guffaws

In orbits of laughter, / The planets collide, / Each jest adds a chapter, / With humor as the guide.

Asteroids bounce and tease, / In cosmic ballet, / With jokes that aim to please, / As they swirl and sway.

Gravity can't hold down / The giggles that rise, / As laughter's renown, / Reaches far and wide.

Amongst the stardust play, / With joy as our base, / We share a light array, / In this vast, funny space.

Eclipse of Exaggeration

The sun took a break, said, 'You'll see me soon,'
But a cat on a roof claimed it danced to the moon.
With shades made of laughter and jokes in a row,
They painted the sky with a dazzling show.

The stars winked and giggled, like kids at a fair,
Painting wild tales with whimsical flair.
A meteor fell, but no wishes were made,
Just endless puns that the comets displayed.

Shooting Star Shenanigans

In a galaxy far, where stardust does roam,
A snail wearing shades built a home out of foam.
He raced with a comet, it turned out to be,
The snail was the fastest, or so he would decree.

With laughter erupting in infinite space,
They held a grand party in a light-speed race.
The punch was a nebula, fizzy and bright,
While aliens cheered, painting laughter in flight.

Interstellar Irony

A wise owl once said, with a wink and a grin,
'Why chase after dreams when the fun's where you've
been?'
With planets in stitches and moons rolling laughs,
They all gathered round for their intergalactic drafts.

A black hole yawned wide, said, 'I'll eat up your fears,
But pass me the jokes; I can't swallow those tears.'
In a dance of mischief, they twirled and they spun,
While gravity giggled, this was just the fun.

Whimsical World Beyond

In a realm where the stars play jump rope with fate,
A jester in space sings, 'It's never too late!'
He juggles the planets with laughter galore,
And the sun joins the chorus, and shimmies for more.

Galaxies twirl in a ballet of light,
While comets crack jokes in the depths of the night.
Each wink from a quasar brings chuckles and glee,
In the world beyond, everyone's silly and free.

Gravity's Giggles

In a realm where tendrils twist,
Laughter's gravity can't be missed.
Stars trip on their own light beams,
As comets share their wildest dreams.

Planets spin in dizzying dance,
With saturnine rings, they take a chance.
A black hole sighs, pulls in the jokes,
While meteors laugh with cosmic folks.

Nebulas bloom in vibrant hues,
Creating giggles that amuse.
Antigravity boots on their feet,
Stumbling through humor so sweet.

In this vast and whimsical scheme,
Every chuckle's a floating beam.
A universe of laughter bright,
In the void, pure joy takes flight.

Space-Time Shenanigans

Wormholes twist, a wild race,
Where time gives humor a funny face.
As planets jostle in absurd glee,
Lightyears bounce like a bouncy bee.

Asteroids chuckle in a parade,
With meteor dust their confetti made.
Galactic pranks under starlit skies,
As gravity winks, and laughter flies.

Aliens swap their silly tales,
Telling jokes with interstellar sales.
Spaceships drip with giggly charms,
While black holes hold hosts in their arms.

In this realm where echoes collide,
Jokes bend time, nowhere to hide.
So let's rocket through the vast unknown,
With every chuckle, we find our throne.

Witty Wormholes

Wormholes wink with playful might,
Swirling humor in the night.
With every twist and every turn,
A cosmic giggle, we still yearn.

Quasars flash with comic flair,
While stardust laughs float in the air.
Gravity pulls, but joy escapes,
Daring us to flip our capes.

In the orbit of a comet's joke,
Laughter rings like a playful poke.
As clowns in space juggle bright stars,
Dance with joy, forget the scars.

Through these portals, we'll drift and glide,
In stellar schemes, a merry ride.
With every laugh, the cosmos sways,
In funny realms, forever stays.

Laughter Among the Stars

Stars gather for a nightly show,
With punchlines that shimmer and glow.
Galaxies chat, their jokes interlace,
Each giggle echoes through boundless space.

Meteor showers rain down laughter,
In swirling chaos, joy's the master.
Planets trade barbs, witty and bright,
As comets crash, igniting the night.

Aliens dance with wobbling grace,
All while jokes orbit in the space.
Gravity struggles, can't hold the glee,
In this realm, we're all wild and free.

With laughter as our guiding star,
We'll journey far, we'll dance, we'll spar.
Through the cosmos, we sing and cheer,
In the universe, humor is near.

Radiant Revelry

Stars are giggling in the night,
Planets dance, what a sight!
Jupiter cracks a dad joke,
While comets make the audience choke.

Aliens join with their best cheer,
Telling tales of the things they fear.
A black hole shrieks, 'Not my style!'
Everyone laughs, it's been a while.

Galaxies swirl in laughter's embrace,
Asteroids tumble, a clumsy race.
With a wink, the sun struts by,
In this laughter, we can fly high.

Humorous Horizons

In the void, where laughter blooms,
Space-time twists, erasing glooms.
Quasars flicker, like bright lights,
Telling tales of wacky flights.

Nebulas burst with colorful jokes,
Shooting stars share laughs, a hoax.
With a punchline, Saturn rings true,
All the planets blush, who knew?

Astro-clowns juggle cosmic pies,
With each slip, the universe sighs.
Universe bursting with glee and jive,
In this hilarity, we thrive.

Planetary Palooza

Moons are spinning, having fun,
While meteors race, not just one.
Black holes giggle at their own blight,
Pulling in punchlines, oh what a sight!

Venus plays on a cosmic guitar,
Singing songs of a distant star.
Mars throws a pie in Uranus' face,
Laughter rings out through space's vast space.

Satellites cheer in a cosmic ballet,
While galaxies spin in a loud hooray.
In the theater of infinite skies,
Where laughter rises, and fun never dies.

Canine Cosmos Comedy

Dogs in space, wearing their hats,
Chasing stars and barking at bats.
With tails a-wagging, they find delight,
In zero-g, they take flight.

Puppies bounce on fine moon dust,
Sharing jokes that are a must.
'Why did the comet cross the ring?'
To fetch the laughs, that's the thing!

With barks that echo through the void,
These furry friends are never annoyed.
In their antics, we find glee,
As they play in the galaxy with me.

Celestial Chuckles

Stars twinkling, winking bright,
The moon might spill a joke tonight.
Galaxies drift in laughter's flow,
As comets dance with a gleeful glow.

Planets grinning, spinning fast,
Orbiting humor, an eternal blast.
A supernova burst of glee,
Shooting stars shout, 'Look at me!'

Black holes swallow all the fun,
Even the sun can't help but run.
Nebulas puff in teasing sighs,
While asteroids wink from the skies.

In the cosmic space of jest,
Every lightyear holds a fest.
So join the laughter, starlit spree,
In the universe's jubilee!

Astrological Amusement

Planets play cards, stakes are high,
Venus bets with a playful sigh.
Mars raises with a cheeky grin,
While Saturn giggles, 'Let the games begin!'

Zodiac signs all gather round,
Finding laughs in the starry sound.
Leo roars, a comedy king,
As Scorpio dives with a funny fling.

Taurus shares tales with a wink,
As Gemini doubles, shares a drink.
Pisces giggles, waves in delight,
Celebrating humor in the night.

A cosmic show where each plays part,
Stars and signs, a brilliant art.
In the galaxy, we find our tune,
Laughter blooms beneath the moon.

The Universe's Jester

The jester juggles stars with flair,
Tickles planets in midair.
Galactic giggles echo loud,
As the cosmos cheers and feels proud.

With jokes that travel light-years wide,
Supernova's burst ignites the tide.
Laughter bounces from rock to star,
Making merry wherever we are.

Asteroids chuckle, rolling free,
Dancing through dark, giddy spree.
Meteor showers rain delight,
As starlight glimmers, sparkling bright.

In this theater of the night,
Every twinkle brings delight.
So here's to jesters, bold and brave,
In the universe, let laughter wave!

Quasars and Quips

Quasars beam with zany wit,
Their cosmic tales make stardust split.
Stellar puns orbit with grace,
While comets race in the laughter chase.

Galaxies swell with smiles and cheer,
Echoes of chuckles ring crystal clear.
A nebula murmurs a soft pun,
Crafting humor with every sun.

Lightyears of laughter spread about,
Twinkling jesters, no hint of doubt.
The cosmos spins in playful jest,
In this vast space, we feel so blessed.

With every quip and a stellar glow,
The universe grins, playfulness flows.
Join the laughter, it's quite the trip,
In this cosmic realm of quips and flips!

Infinity's Improv

In a galaxy full of jest,
Stars giggle in their cosmic vest.
Planets spin in laughter bright,
While comets wink, a playful sight.

Black holes hide their cosmic grin,
Swallowing jokes where they begin.
Nebulas puff with giggling gas,
Echoes of chuckles as they pass.

Aliens dance, with silly moves,
Making stardust as laughter grooves.
Martians tell tales of Earthly woes,
Their punchlines land with cosmic prose.

A supernova bursts with delight,
Lights up the night, a funny flight.
In the humor of space, we all find,
Infinite laughs that are truly kind.

Spirited Space Soirée

Gather round in the twinkling haze,
Where echoes of laughter fill the space.
Galactic jesters take center stage,
With stars in their eyes, they engage.

Wormholes twist with weekend plans,
Time travel jokes fill up the stands.
Comets break into fits of glee,
As universes blend so carefree.

Uranus jokes about its rings,
While Saturn spins tales that have wings.
Laughter rockets to the Milky Way,
As starlight shimmers, keeping gloom at bay.

Meteor showers shower us all,
With giggles galore, they never fall.
In this soirée of light and cheer,
The cosmos stands up, and we all cheer.

Cosmic Comedians

Stars telling jokes in a glowing chat,
Punchlines flying—imagine that!
A nebula trips on its own two feet,
Cracking itself up as it sways to the beat.

Quasars beam with bright, bold style,
With cosmic quips they make us smile.
Even black holes can take a jest,
Flipping humor from east to west.

Asteroids tumble in fits of glee,
Stones of laughter float aimlessly.
Space dust tickles the end of a joke,
With every chuckle, the universe stoked.

Galaxies swirl in a comedic spin,
Where everyone knows that laughter's the win.
In the vastness, we find our place,
With cosmic comedians full of grace.

Humor on the Horizon

On the edge of space, where starlight bends,
Life's a punchline that never ends.
Across the cosmos, laughter streams,
In the silence, humor gleams.

Astrophysicists cracking their codes,
While planets tease with their wobbly loads.
The universe giggles and sways in time,
With every quip, it bursts into rhyme.

Satellites spin in their playful flight,
Throwing back jests, both day and night.
From the dark void, a chuckle rings,
As stars play tag, doing silly things.

In every corner, jokes are found,
An interstellar laugh that knows no bound.
Up high in space, where hilarity soars,
Humor on the horizon, forever explores.

Celestial Stand-Up

Stars in a spotlight, bright and bold,
Crack jokes about black holes, untold.
Planets spin laughter, round and round,
In the vastness of space, joy abound.

Comets with punchlines shoot through the night,
Laughing at meteors, what a sight!
Galactic giggles echo so far,
While aliens chuckle in their bizarre.

Nebulas bloom with wit on display,
Tickling each quasar in playful array.
Astrophysics laughs at gravity's pull,
As cosmic jesters keep the world full.

In the void where time and space align,
Every laugh feels like a twist of time.
Under the moon's gaze, all unite,
In this universe, comedy takes flight.

Humor in the Helix

DNA and jokes twist in a dance,
Spirals of laughter, take a chance.
Cells burst with humor, vibrant and spry,
Life's so funny, just watch it fly.

Atoms collide with punchlines anew,
Quarks giggle along, who knew?
Electrons buzzing in comedic delight,
Creating smiles through the darkest night.

Genetic comedy, nature's own glee,
Evolution's staging a stand-up spree.
Each chromosome's a joke waiting to land,
In the tapestry of life, nothing is bland.

Biologists chuckle, with petri dish crowds,
Jokes about science, they roar out loud.
In this helix of humor, all are embraced,
In the circle of life, laughter is traced.

Joviality Among the Planets

Mercury's racing, it's quick on the laugh,
While Neptune tells tales of a watery path.
Earth spins with jokes, in vibrant hues,
Banter flows freely, like morning dew.

Jupiter's storms swirl joyfully round,
While Venus spreads love, a chuckle profound.
Saturn spins rings, each one a jest,
A cosmic roulette, humor at its best.

Mars joins the fray with a red-cheeked grin,
Witty banter flows like the tides within.
Uranus chuckles, a laugh so surreal,
Making fun of the sun, oh, the appeal!

Through the solar system, laughter does soar,
As planets unite in a raucous roar.
Celestial beings, together they play,
In this realm of humor, forever they stay.

The Asteroid Antics

Asteroids tumble, they trip and they fall,
Dodging the sun, a cosmic free-for-all.
Bouncing in orbits, they play tag with speed,
In this rocky playhouse, laughter's the creed.

Fragments of fun, scattered in space,
Each rock a comedian, finding their place.
Cracking up Saturn, with sly little pranks,
Rolling in laughter, forming new ranks.

Comet tails flicker in a witty display,
With every bright flash, they brighten the day.
Galaxies watch the hilarity unfold,
In this endless theater, a joy to behold.

So heed the asteroids, as they swirl and glide,
Join in their antics, let laughter be your guide.
In the depths of the cosmos, where silliness reigns,
The universe chuckles, while joy entertains.

Black Star Blooper

In a galaxy far, far away,
A star dropped its jokes on display.
Planets laughed till they spun,
Even black holes thought it was fun.

Nebulas winked with delight,
Stardust danced in sheer light.
Asteroids chuckled, quite bold,
Creating laughter untold.

A comet zipped by with a quip,
It swirled, did a loop, and a flip.
Space was filled with riotous cheer,
As beings laughed without fear.

Supernovae glimmered with glee,
While cosmic clowns brewed up tea.
The universe grinned wide and bright,
In that starry comedy night.

Antics Beyond the Atmosphere

Out beyond the clouds' embrace,
Jesters float in a merry race.
They toss starry pies and play,
In this vast sky where they sway.

Galactic giggles echo loud,
As aliens form a silly crowd.
Wormholes twist in laughter's grip,
Stars gather round for the trip.

Meteorites juggle and jest,
Each punchline a quirky test.
Even satellites can't resist,
Join the fun, they simply can't mist.

In the void where silence lay,
Laughter thunders night and day.
Strange rhythms in the astral breeze,
Invite all beings to giggle with ease.

Jokes in the Jetstream

High above where the eagles soar,
Jetstreams whisper jokes galore.
Each gust brings a punchline fresh,
A laugh building up like a mesh.

Airplanes buzz with comic flair,
Their wings tickled by the air.
Clouds take a tumble, roll on the floor,
As they chuckle forevermore.

Stratosphere's where the laughter grows,
As gravity plays tag with those.
Skydivers fall with a grin so wide,
In the heavens, joy can't hide.

Twilight skies glow with mirth,
While comets parade through their birth.
In this high-flying comedy show,
Laughter whirls, it's all aglow.

Cosmic Chucklefest

In the depths of the endless night,
Stars gather round for sheer delight.
A festival of chuckles and fun,
Where every cosmic creature can run.

Quasars blink with witty flair,
While planets trip in the air.
Gravity drops a beat so sweet,
As space-time dances on its feet.

Space-time jesters roam the void,
Galactic silliness, never cloyed.
Black holes spin tales, hard to beat,
Metallic beams tap their feet.

Superheroes of humor unite,
In a universe painted bright.
Join the giggles, spread the laughs,
In this expanse of cosmic drafts.

Satire in the Stars

In orbits where laughter spins,
Planets chuckle, it's where chaos begins.
Asteroids tell jokes with a punch,
While aliens gather for a quirky brunch.

The moons roll their eyes at the sun's bright jokes,
As dark matter giggles, and black holes poke.
Constellations dance with a wink and a grin,
Creating a comedy show where all stars win.

Galactic puns echo through the vastness of night,
With comet tails flicking, oh what a sight!
Space dust sparkles like sequins on stage,
Inviting each critter to join in this page.

So tune in your ears to the whispers of space,
Where absurdity thrives in a galactic embrace.
Laughter's the language of stellar delight,
As we float through the cosmos, hearts feeling light.

Interstellar Improv

In the theater of endless night,
Stars take center stage under moonlight.
Black holes pull punchlines from the void,
While comets prance, utterly overjoyed.

Planets warmed by the laugh track's glow,
As meteors crash with a splendid show.
Gravity's laws twisted into fun,
Jokes fly faster than the speed of a pun.

Martians in wigs dance in zero G,
They tumble and twirl, what a sight to see!
Galaxies spin to the beat of their cheer,
The universe giggles, a grand cavalier.

Every quasar beams, another scene shines,
In a cosmic theater where humor aligns.
Comedic chaos in spacetime's embrace,
Forever together in this joyous place.

Cosmic Clowning

Juggling stars with a cosmic flair,
Clowns in spacesuits float through the air.
Planets giggle as they swirl and spin,
Creating a circus where laughter begins.

Gravity pulls on a ballooning moon,
As nebulae burst out in a merry tune.
Shooting stars laugh at their speedy plight,
Zooming through space in a whirlwind of light.

Aliens honk on laughable horns,
While space whales sing of absurd woes and scorns.
The universe watches, amused and awake,
As comets trip over their own silly wake.

Join the parade of this galactic jest,
Where every quirk gets a lively fest.
In the fabric of space, mirth is the muse,
As we all share in this celestial cruise.

Side-Splitters on Saturn

Around the rings, they gather and cheer,
Side-splitters floating, there's laughter here.
Saturn's friends joke in a swirling race,
As giggles erupt from the vast open space.

With moons telling tales of the silliest kinds,
While swirling gas clouds twirl in playful binds.
The dance of the orbs sets the scene ablaze,
Creating a whirlpool of laughter and praise.

Meteor showers rain down witty quips,
As warriors of humor, they flip and they dip.
The gas giants chuckle, the stardust admires,
Each cosmic punchline ignites new desires.

Fly high with the jesters who expand the sky,
In the heavyweight laughter of Saturn's sly eye.
Join the parade, let your spirits unfold,
In the rings of this planet, pure joy to behold.

Jovian Jollity

A giant storm with a wink so wide,
Jokes float by on a swirling tide.
Galactic giggles echo far and near,
As planets chuckle, it's clear we're here.

Stars in tuxedos dance in the night,
With each punchline, they shine so bright.
Moons trade quips as they waltz through space,
In this vast realm, we find our place.

Asteroid clowns tumble through the void,
With slapstick joy that can't be toyed.
Nebulae paint a canvas of cheer,
In this orbit, laughter is dear.

So grab a comet, join the parade,
In this universe, no joy will fade.
With every twist of the cosmic plot,
We find the humor that can't be bought.

Laughter Without Limits

In the depths of space, laughter rings,
Galaxies sway as the humor swings.
No boundaries here in this jester's den,
Where the punchlines echo and then begin again.

Aliens munch on popcorn delight,
Giggling stars in the velvet night.
Comets streak by, tails ablaze,
Joining the fun in whimsical ways.

A black hole yawns with a snicker so deep,
Sucking in worries, laughs, and sweet sleep.
Divine hilarity, an endless spree,
In this universe, wild and free.

As supernovas burst with glee,
We all join in the jubilee.
So laugh aloud, let your spirit soar,
In this limitless realm, there's always more.

Astral Amusement

With a wink, the sun beams down its light,
Tickling the stars in the dark of night.
A laughing moon spins tales so grand,
In this celestial comedy land.

Saturn's rings, a jester's attire,
Twist and twirl, they never tire.
Each planet shares its own goofy fact,
In this astral show, fun's intact.

Gravity's pull can't hold back the joy,
Meteor showers, a festive ploy.
With each twinkling star, a wink and nod,
This universe laughs, and it feels so odd.

Bring your own punchline, join in the fun,
With cosmic chuckles, we unite as one.
So let's orbit round with smiles in tow,
In this comedy void, we steal the show.

Intergalactic Improv

On a stage of stars, they strut and play,
Quick-witted aliens lead the way.
With every ad-lib, the cosmos grins,
As laughter erupts, the fun begins.

Planets pitch in, each on their cue,
Creating a scene that's weird and new.
Galactic laughter spills over the rim,
The universe jokes, and we all join in.

A supernova pops, a punchline hit,
As cosmic creators don't dare to quit.
With black holes and quarks, they take the stage,
Crafting a show that defies the age.

So let's catch a ride on this hilarious wave,
No script required, just be brave.
In this improv galore, we find our delight,
As stardust chuckles fill up the night.

Comet's Comic Relief

A comet zooms by, tail in the air,
Telling jokes 'bout stars without a care.
Planets crack up, rolling in glee,
As the space dust giggles in harmony.

Asteroids dance, their rhythm so wild,
Floating through space like a playful child.
Nebulas chuckle, their colors so bright,
In the vacuum of night, they spark with delight.

Black holes grin, with a mischievous twinkle,
Swallowing laughter, it makes the hearts crinkle.
Galaxies swirl in a spiraled embrace,
In this stellar stage, there's no need for grace.

So float on, dear friends, and laugh 'neath the skies,
Where the cosmos delights with its limitless highs.
With each twinkling star, there's a giggle to share,
In this universe grand, humor's everywhere!

A Cosmic Caper

Venus wore shades, a diva in space,
Jupiter juggled, keeping up the pace.
Saturn's rings chimed, a musical tune,
As Mars did a shuffle beneath the bright moon.

A starlet named Nova, in glittery dress,
Tells tales of mischief, of laughter no less.
With cosmic confetti, they dance through the night,
Creating a show that's pure delight.

In some far-off corner, a quasar is sly,
Cracking up space with its twinkling eye.
While comets collide with a splash and a wink,
In the theater of space, we all stop to think.

So gather 'round, pals, and let your hearts soar,
In this caper of stars, you'll find laughter galore.
With a bounce in your step and a smile on your face,
Join this whirling feel-good, infinite space!

Whimsical Wonders of the Void

In the vast dark, where neither is near,
Wonders unfold, bringing laughter and cheer.
Galactic giggles echo through the night,
As the universe twirls in sheer delight.

Shooting stars prank, racing to and fro,
While space-time bends in a cosmic show.
With critters of light, they twist and they spin,
Bringing joy and laughter from deep within.

A nebula sneezes, releasing bright hues,
Creating a riot of shimmering views.
In this playground of stars, each moment we share,
Its whimsical wonders fill us with care.

So let's raise a toast to the night so grand,
To the laughter that dances across every land.
With every bright spark that's born from the void,
In this playful expanse, we're forever overjoyed!

Orbiting Oddities

Round and round in a curious dance,
Quirky planets make us glance.
With orbits so odd, they twirl and spin,
In this funny vastness, laughter begins.

Uranus winks, such a cheeky sight,
While Neptune hums a tune through the night.
Each star plays a part in this tale so bizarre,
As they gather 'round for a night at the bar.

Meteor showers, like confetti they fall,
Making wishes that echo to us all.
In this celestial circus, there's magic abloom,
With humor that piques from the dark, endless room.

So let's orbit together, oddities in hand,
Through this whimsical space, oh so unplanned.
In every bright twinkle, a chuckle's in store,
In this vast universe, who could ask for more?

Celestial Comedy Chronicles

In the depths of night, stars tease and twirl,
Laughter echoes high, as planets unfurl.
A comet zips by, with a wink and a grin,
Telling jokes to the moons, where laughter begins.

Galaxies spin with a humorous spin,
Neptune jokes with Mars, what a funny kin!
Black holes just chuckle, with a deep, dark glee,
Sucking in laughter, as it swirls with the sea.

Jupiter rumbles, a giant of jest,
While Saturn's rings dance, they're simply the best.
Quasars beam bright, like a spotlight on stage,
Telling tales of the universe, page by page.

So let's toast to the stars, in this grand night sky,
Where laughter's the fuel, and goodwill's the high.
With humor as vast as the universe wide,
We giggle with glee, as we take a ride.

Galactic Laughs

In a nebula's glow, jokes start to bloom,
Space dust chuckles, dispelling the gloom.
Aliens gather, with green skin and eyes,
Swapping punchlines beneath cosmic skies.

Orbiting planets roll on the floor,
While asteroids dance, asking for more.
Light-years apart, wit travels at speed,
With each giggle shared, our laughter is freed.

Supernovae burst, like confetti in air,
As the universe jokes, we can't help but share.
Even the sun, with its dazzling flair,
Offers up puns that are hotter than air.

So come one, come all, to this stellar show,
Where laughter's the currency that helps us grow.
In this cosmic expanse, there's room for delight,
As we revel in humor, through day and through night.

Stardust Stand-Up

A shooting star shot by, with a punchline so bright,
It tickled a neutron, who exploded with light.
Galactic giggles echo through the dark,
While quipsters assemble in this cosmic park.

Black holes may swallow, but they don't take jest,
They ponder the punchlines, wishing for rest.
Each twinkling star joins in on the fun,
With stories and gags, we're never outdone.

Asteroids roll in, with a bump and a crash,
Delivering puns, in a speedy flash.
The cosmos performs, a show without end,
Where laughter's a thread that all beings can send.

So grab your seat now, the universe waits,
For punchlines that swirl through the uncharted states.
With stardust and smiles, let's keep the delight,
In this endless expanse, we'll laugh through the night.

Interstellar Jest

Far beyond our world, in spaces unknown,
Neon comets giggle, with a humor of their own.
Planets engage in a raucous debate,
Over whose jokes are the best—oh, it's great!

Space whales sing songs of whimsical tales,
While distant quasars flash like comedy trails.
Galactic giggles ripple through the void,
As laughter's the spark that can't be destroyed.

Wormholes twist funny, like a cosmic slide,
In a supernova's glow, our grins can't hide.
Eclipse of the moon? A setup for fun,
As shadows play tricks when the day's almost done.

So come, let's unite under starlight and cheer,
For joy in the journey, let's make that clear.
In this vast universe, we're all part of the jest,
With humor connecting us—truly the best.

Quantum Quirks

In glimmers of stars, the jokes take flight,
Particles waltz in whimsical light.
Entanglement tangles in laughable ways,
Time's just a punchline that bends and sways.

Quarks doing stand-up, what a wild scene,
With photons giggling, the laughs intervene.
Gravity's pull can't keep down a grin,
In the dance of the cosmos, we're all kin.

Sassy Satellites

Orbiting planets with style and sass,
These cheeky moons enjoy a good pass.
They throw shade on comets with comical flair,
Whirling past asteroids, giving them dare.

From Mars to Neptune, they strut and they tease,
While laughing at meteors like playful bees.
Each rotation a punchline, each eclipse a jest,
In the vastness of space, they know they're the best.

Nebulosity of Nonsense

In clouds of color, the absurd does bloom,
Where giggles and gags fill the cosmic room.
Stars sneeze confetti that dances around,
While celestial beings create laughter sound.

With a wink and a twist, the universe sings,
Filling the void with ridiculous things.
Supernova parties explode in delight,
As laughter spreads through the velvet night.

Comic Without Borders

Galaxies grouping in comedic embrace,
No limits on laughter, all cultures in place.
From Earth to Andromeda, humor abounds,
Echoing softly in interstellar sounds.

Punchlines in languages no one can trace,
Universal chuckles fill outer space.
With space-faring jesters that cross light-years wide,
In the vastness of nothing, joy won't hide.

Jovian Jocularities

In the clouds of gas, the laughter swirls,
Jovian jesters dance and twirl.
With storms that speak like witty friends,
Their humor stretches, never ends.

A lightning bolt, a punchline bright,
Jupiter chuckles in the night.
Winds whip tales of cosmic fun,
Where each new jest is just begun.

They say there's life in every storm,
With gags and jests a swirling norm.
In the vastness, humor's key,
Making even gas giants glee.

Oh, to be part of that grand show,
Where every quasar puts on a glow.
In Jovian realms, all's a delight,
With laughter echoing through the night.

Saturn's Sarcasm

Rings of laughter spin and spin,
Where Saturn grins with a cheeky chin.
Dropping jokes, like icy gems,
The Saturnian stand-up never pretends.

Each moon a fan with a chuckle and clap,
While comets tell tales with a zany rap.
"Why did the ring cross the space?" they tease,
"To orbit you better, if you please!"

With playful wisecracks, they float in the void,
In this great emptiness, humor's enjoyed.
Saturn's scenes are never mundane,
Jokes roll like planets on paths of the insane.

So gather 'round, in the starlit night,
Where Saturn's wit brings pure delight.
In the spectacle of stars, all seem okay,
In the laughter of space, we whimsically stay.

Lunar Laugh Fest

On the surface of the moon, so pale and bright,
Laughter echoes in the muted light.
With craters like smiles, wide and round,
A festival of giggles is easily found.

Astronauts do stand-up in gravity's line,
Floating jokes, one-liners, all divine.
"Why did the moon hide behind the sun?"
"Too bright for humor, that's no fun!"

In lunar shadows, their antics delight,
With comedic quirks lighting up the night.
Earthlings chuckle at the scene so absurd,
As laughter rises, unfiltered, unheard.

So come join the feast where jokes take flight,
In the celestial dome, we bask in delight.
Under the stars, where mirth can soar,
The lunar laugh fest forevermore.

Celestial Comedy Circuit

Stars twinkle like spotlights on the stage,
Where comets perform in cosmic rage.
Galactic jokes from the depths of space,
A riot of fun in this spacious place.

Planets rotate, applause all around,
A circuit of laughter profoundly sound.
Supernovae put on a show so bright,
With explosive puns that light up the night.

The universe's jesters never tire,
With witticisms that catch like fire.
From black holes to nebulas, all join in,
In this stellar club, let the humor begin!

So beam up your smile as you drift in flight,
In the cosmic embrace, everything feels right.
With stars as our audience, we take our bows,
In the great comedy circuit, laughter endows.

Humor from the Heavens

Stars giggle in the night,
As planets dance in delight.
Comets wisecrack on the way,
While meteors laugh and play.

Galaxies spin with a grin,
Asteroids chuckle where they've been.
Wormholes whisper silly jokes,
And nebulae twirl with happy folks.

Laughter echoes through the space,
A punchline floats in endless grace.
Galactic jesters, bright and bold,
Share tales of wonders yet untold.

In the universe's grand design,
Every quasar leads a punchline.
With each burst, laughter blooms,
As joy erupts from cosmic rooms.

Planetary Puns

Why did Jupiter call the Moon?
To share a joke about a cartoon!
Mars winked, saying it's no crime,
To laugh at life, one pun at a time.

Saturn's rings, a circus feat,
Hold tales that make us all repeat.
Venus blushes, a joke to tell,
As the sun beams down, all is well.

Mercury zips with a witty quip,
While asteroids take a comic trip.
Pluto's punchlines, though small in scale,
Bring laughter bright, they never fail.

Uranus chuckles with a twist,
Telling tales that just can't be missed.
In this orbit of giggles and glee,
The whole universe is one big spree.

Supernova Snickers

When stars explode with great delight,
It's not just light; it's humor bright.
A supernova cracks a grin,
Saying, "See, let the fun begin!"

Galactic giggles light the void,
Where laughter thumps and joy's enjoyed.
Each explosion brings a burst of cheer,
As cosmic jesters fill the sphere.

Nebulae puff out clouds of fun,
Reminding all to laugh and run.
Shooting stars drop punchlines low,
In the night as bright dreams glow.

Star clusters chuckle in rehearsals,
Sharing jokes about parallel universals.
In this playground of the wide night sky,
Even light years can't hold back a sigh.

Black Hole Banter

Deep in the void, where time stands still,
A black hole's mouth gives quite a thrill.
It swallows jokes, yet spits them back,
With a grin that's never off track.

What did the black hole say to the sun?
"You shine bright, but I still have fun!"
With twists and turns, it plays around,
In its pull, all humor is found.

Stars get lost, but never the jokes,
As the universe laughs with playful pokes.
Event horizons hold laughter tight,
In the whisper of the endless night.

So dive right into that cosmic delight,
Where banter spins and stars ignite.
In every swirl, there's mischief and cheer,
Even in darkness, joy is here!

Celestial Chuckles

Stars twinkle like jesters, bright,
Asteroids dance in pure delight.
Planets spin with a silly grace,
Galaxies giggle in their place.

Comets zoom with a whoosh and zoom,
While black holes swallow up the gloom.
Supernovas blast out their cheer,
Echoes of laughter, far and near.

In moonbeams, echoes of joy arise,
Cosmic quirks under velvet skies.
Quasars beam a humorous spark,
Lighting up the vast and dark.

Astrophysicists crack a smile,
Measuring distances with style.
In the void, where humor thrives,
Count the laughs, that's how it survives.

Orbiting Humor

Silly satellites spin around,
Joking with moons without a sound.
Winking stars share a funny tale,
While comets giggle, leaving a trail.

Gravity pulls on punchlines tight,
As meteors fall in silly flight.
Astrology predicts laughter bright,
Stars align for a cosmic night.

Black holes with a cheeky grin,
Swallowing light, just for the win.
Nebulas puff like cotton candy,
Spreading joy far and handy.

Each orbit holds a joke untold,
The universe is gleefully bold.
Orbiting humor, a grand parade,
In this vastness, fun will never fade.

Nebula of Jokes

In colorful clouds, wit does bloom,
Punchlines burst from the cosmic gloom.
Twinkling stars, a sparkling crowd,
They chuckle softly, feeling proud.

Planets swirl in laughter's embrace,
Echoing joy through boundless space.
Asteroids roll with comical flair,
Wobbling, laughing without a care.

Galactic giggles fill the night,
Spilling stardust, oh what a sight!
Meteors streak with jokes in tow,
Through the nebula, the laughter flows.

A supernova bursts, how divine,
Sending shimmers and jokes that shine.
In the vastness, humor's a guide,
Brightening the cosmos far and wide.

Universal Punchlines

In the vastness, jokes take flight,
Across the cosmos, pure delight.
Stars align in a punchy set,
While comets race, you'll never forget.

The moon whispers a punchline sweet,
While sunbeams dance on playful feet.
Each quasar's wink spreads joy anew,
Fabric of space bursts into a view.

Gravity's pull on funny affairs,
Spinning tales with cosmic flares.
Galaxies join in the uproar,
With laughter echoing evermore.

Time's a joker with tricks to share,
In this universe, all's made fair.
Punchlines weave through the endless night,
A universal giggle, pure delight.

Comedic Constellations

Stars gather round, a joke to share,
Nebulas giggle, float without a care.
Planets burst forth with playful quips,
Creating laughter in their cosmic trips.

A meteor stumbled, tripped on air,
Said, "Why so serious? I'm just a flare!"
Galaxies twirled, in a cosmic dance,
Spreading joy and a wide-eyed glance.

Wormholes whisper, secrets untold,
Each poke of humor, pure gold to behold.
Gravity chuckles, pulls us near,
In this vast universe, we conquer fear.

So grab a seat among the stars,
Where puns are plenty, and laughter spars.
The night is young, the humor bright,
Join the delight in the cosmic light.

Jovian Jests

Jove laughs deep with his thunderous roar,
While moons make faces, begging for more.
Clouds play tricks with a wink and a nod,
In the realm of gas giants, humor's a prod.

Saturn spins tales with its rings so wide,
Telling all planets, "Come take a ride!"
Uranus chuckles, a twist in its spin,
Saying, "I'm the funny one, let the laughs begin!"

Each storm a punchline, swirling so free,
As comet tails giggle, can't you see?
The laughter erupts, from pole to pole,
In this jovial expanse, we lose all control.

So raise your glasses to Saturn's rings,
For each joke it tells, a laughter that sings.
In a gas giant's grip, fun covers all,
Bringing the universe in a jolly sprawl.

Lightyear Laughter

Across the void where light travels swift,
Stars hold a gathering, passing a gift.
They trade jokes with speed of a flash,
Laughter echoes, a brilliant crash.

Distances fade where the humor dares,
Galaxies giggling, sharing their airs.
A lightyear's worth of puns on display,
As space itself chuckles, night into day.

Wormholes wink, carrying gags galore,
Beyond the horizons, where jokes can soar.
With every pulse of a quasar's light,
Laughter unites what's distant from sight.

So tune your ears to the cosmic sound,
For joy is a language where love is found.
In the vastness of space, we're never alone,
For humor connects us, wherever we roam.

Comet's Caustic Comeback

A comet zoomed by, its tail in a swirl,
Shouting out jokes as it made the world hurl.
"Why did the asteroid cross the sky?
To dodge the punchline, oh my, oh my!"

With a sparkle and gleam, it twirled with glee,
Chasing dusk's laughter, as bright as can be.
'Round the sun's orbit, jokes took flight,
Each stellar pun lighting up the night.

Lunar friends listened, eyes wide with cheer,
As comets cracked jokes that all would hear.
"Why don't aliens ever lose at hide?
Because they know the stars, too well they hide!"

In the wake of its path, the cosmos would grin,
With every new punchline, life would begin.
So catch the next comet, and join in the fun,
For the universe beams when we've all made one.

Stellar Satire

In the depths of space, a joke takes flight,
Aliens chuckle at the stars so bright.
One star said, "Why so serious, friend?"
The universe winked; the laughter won't end.

Comets zoom by with a playful grace,
Telling puns as they race through space.
Black holes laugh, 'We suck in the light!'
But even they know how to take flight.

Planets spin, sharing tales of glee,
One says, "I'm rounder than your galaxy!"
Saturn's rings laugh, "We're quite the design!"
As they twirl and dance, oh what a time!

In the cosmic lounge, a nebula sings,
Jokes about gravity and other such things.
Life's a riot when the stars all align,
So grab a seat – it's comedy time!

Quasar Quips

Bright quasars flash with a wink and a grin,
Telling tales of space as they spin.
In a galaxy far, there's a giggle or two,
Where laughter expands like the universe blue.

Supernova laughs, don't know when to quit,
Says, "I just exploded, but isn't it lit?"
Stars trade their jokes over coffee and tea,
With laughter so loud, it's a cosmic spree!

"Why did the asteroid break up?" one cries,
"Too many collisions, it wanted to fly!"
The meteors roar, their humor on fire,
As the planets all join in, rising higher.

Comets and asteroids, a rowdy bunch,
Sharing secrets of space over a brunch.
"Why do stars never get lost in the dark?"
They twinkle and laugh; oh what a spark!

Astrological Antics

Zodiac signs gather, what a strange crew,
With giggles and chuckles that echo so true.
Aries cracks jokes about leaving in haste,
While Taurus munches snacks with unhurried taste.

Gemini's puns take the crowd by surprise,
"I can be two things, just look in my eyes!"
Cancer tells tales of the moon's silly prance,
While Leo roars, "I'm here for the dance!"

Virgo's precision meets humor's loose threads,
"Why be so serious when you can have spreads?"
Libra's balance, of laughter and cheer,
Brings harmony to all, everyone here.

Sagittarius shoots arrows of glee,
While Capricorn's punchlines climb ever so high.
Aquarius beams, sharing dreams in a whirl,
With Pisces swimming through jokes like a pearl!

Laughter Across Lightyears

Across lightyears, laughter transcends the night,
Stars giggle and dance, such a beautiful sight.
Cosmic puppets play on the strings of the sky,
As comets bring joy, and the sun beams a sly.

"What's an alien's favorite candy?" they tease,
"Milky Ways, of course, they're sure to please!"
Eclipses and Nova bring chuckles anew,
In the vastness of space, laughter's a brew.

The cosmos is filled with jokes interstellar,
As satellites spin and spin like a teller.
Pulsars stutter with laughter, a rhythmic delight,
While moons wink at stars in the velvety night.

Join in the fun, leave your worries behind,
For laughter is timeless – a gift for mankind.
So let's toast to the heavens with giggles and cheer,
In the grand cosmic stage, let joy persevere!